John and Mary Gribbin

CURIE
(1867–1934)
in 90 minutes

Constable · London

First published in Great Britain 1997
by Constable and Company Limited
3 The Lanchesters, 162 Fulham Palace Road
London W6 9ER
Copyright © John and Mary Gribbin 1997
The right of John and Mary Gribbin to be
identified as authors
of this work has been asserted by them
in accordance with the Copyright,
Designs and Patents Act 1988
ISBN 0 09 477020 4
Set in Linotype Sabon by
Rowland Phototypesetting Ltd,
Bury St Edmunds, Suffolk
Printed in Great Britain by
St Edmundsbury Press Ltd,
Bury St Edmunds, Suffolk

A CIP catalogue record for this book
is available from the British Library

Contents

Curie in context

Marie Curie achieved great things in science partly because she was a very good scientist, partly because she was in the right place at the right time, and in no small measure because of her background as an educated Polish woman determined to make her mark in spite of the oppression of her country by its neighbours. You had to be tough to achieve anything in the circumstances in which Marya Sklodowska, as she was then called, was brought up. But if you were tough, those circumstances could make you tougher still; the difficulties she later encountered in Paris, which would have daunted most people, she overcame almost as a matter of routine.

Marya was born on 7 November 1867, in Warsaw. At that time, Poland technically did not exist. At the end of the eighteenth century the country had been divided up between Russia, Prussia and Austria; the part the Sklodowskis lived in was, in 1867, a province of Russia. Following two desperate and bloody uprisings (in 1830 and 1863), at the time Marya was born and throughout her early life that part of Poland was undergoing a process of Russification. So severe was it that not only was Russian the official language but Polish could be taught in schools only as a foreign language – with the teaching being done in Russian.

Some Poles died in the uprisings; thousands (including the brother of Marya's mother) were transported to Siberia by the Russians; tens of thousands (including the brother of Marya's father) fled into exile, many in France. Wherever possible, official positions in Polish society were filled by Russians, a move which was to have a big effect on Marya's life. Even the street signs and shop signs were written in Cyrillic characters. In the last third of the nineteenth century, open insurrection was no longer a feasible way for the Poles to throw off the Russian yoke. But there were, as we shall see, other ways of fighting the oppression, and Marya was hardened in the process.

Scientifically speaking, Marya was born at just the right time to participate in one of the greatest of scientific revolutions. It was at the end of the nineteenth century that people began to probe (at first unknowingly) processes that go on in the hearts of atoms. When Marya was born, atoms were not yet firmly established in the minds of all scientists as real entities. The first key development (the first chronologically; as far as understanding the atom was concerned, it came too soon and out of sequence) was in 1895, when the German physicist Wilhelm Röntgen discovered X-rays.

Like many physicists in the 1890s, Röntgen was experimenting with the radiation that emanates from a wire carrying an electric current inside an evacuated tube – so-called cathode rays. When these 'rays' (now known to be a steam of electrons) strike a material object, the collision can produce a secondary radiation which is invisible, and can be detected only by its effect on photographic plates or film, or on a fluorescent screen, which produces flashes of light when struck by energetic radiation. Röntgen happened to have a fluorescent screen lying near his cathode-ray experiment, and spotted the tell-tale flashes. He quickly identified the cause to be this secondary radiation, which he called X-radiation, because x is traditionally the unknown quantity in a mathematical equation.

The nature of the cathode rays themselves was

revealed by a series of experiments carried out by J.J. Thomson's team at the Cavendish Laboratory in England, completed in 1897. Cathode rays had been discovered in the middle of the nineteenth century, and were first investigated in some detail by William Crookes, in the 1870s; Crookes even noticed that photographic plates kept near his cathode-ray tubes became fogged, but did not follow up on the discovery. It was Thomson who established that cathode rays are a stream of negatively charged particles (electrons). He went on to show that they are tiny pieces that have somehow been chipped off, or escaped from, atoms, leaving behind most of the mass of the atom (with a residual positive charge) as a positive ion. You start with an electrically neutral atom, remove a little something carrying negative charge, and a positively charged ion is left behind. Not only did this demonstrate the reality of atoms, it showed that they were not the ultimate building-blocks of matter, but were made up of yet smaller entities which did interesting things in their own right. A whole new world was opened up to scientific investigation.

In February 1896, in between the discovery of

X-rays and the identification of the true nature of cathode rays, Henri Becquerel, working in Paris, discovered radioactivity. The nature of the discovery also lay somewhere in between Röntgen's rather serendipitous discovery of X-rays and Thomson's thorough series of carefully planned experiments that led to the identification of the electron. The story has often been told of how Becquerel was actually trying to find out whether some sort of X-ray like activity might be stimulated in (among other things) uranium salts by the action of sunlight, in a process similar to phosphorescence. As one of a series of similar tests, he prepared a photographic plate wrapped in black paper which he intended to place under a dish containing the uranium salts in the sunlight, to see whether this might lead to some radiation from the uranium passing through the paper and fogging the plate. Because it was cloudy, the experiment stood (with the dish of uranium salts on top of the wrapped photographic plate) shut up in a cupboard for two days. Then, more or less acting on a whim, Becquerel developed the photographic plate anyway, and found that it had been fogged. Uranium produced some form of penetrating radiation whether or not it was exposed to sunlight.

There was an enormous and immediate fuss made about X-rays, which were perceived to have immediate application both in medicine and (at the time) in entertainment, for demonstrations in parlours and theatres. There was an enthusiastic response in scientific circles to Thomson's work on electrons suggesting that the atom possessed internal structure. But at first few people knew quite what to make of radioactivity (as Becquerel's discovery became known). It was just the right sort of thing for a young researcher to take up as the basis for work leading to a doctorate. And at the end of 1897, Marie Curie, as she was by then known, was just the right sort of young researcher to take up the task.

Life and Work

The best description of Marya's parents is 'faded gentry'. On the side of her father, Wladislaw, the Sklodowskis came from the region of Sklody, to the north of Warsaw, where little more than a hundred years before her birth her direct ancestors had owned several hundred acres of land. On the side of her mother, Bronislawa Boguska, the family had declined from running their own estates to managing land for wealthier families. Both Marya's parents were teachers. Wladislaw specialized in science and mathematics, and worked within the official system, very much under the control (and at the mercy) of the Russians. Bronislawa ran a private school for girls, which, since girls (especially Polish girls in the Russian Empire) were not expected by the official authorities to go on to higher education, or do anything much except become good little housewives, fell outside the Russian system. Although this had its advantages, there was a downside. After the uprising of 1863 such schools came under intense scrutiny, since, being run by Poles for Poles, they were thought to be (and indeed were) potential breeding-grounds for sedition.

Wladislaw and Bronislawa married in 1860. At first they lived in an apartment above Bronislawa's school, near the centre of Warsaw. Over the next seven years, while continuing her work as head of the school, Bronislawa produced five children – Zofia, Jozef, Bronislawa, Helena and, in 1867, last of all, Marya. In 1868, however, Wladislaw was promoted to the post of assistant director of a high school (*gymnasium*) on the western side of Warsaw, and Bronislawa was able to give up her post. The family moved into an apartment at Wladislaw's new school, on the edge of the Jewish quarter, where Marya spent her early years.

Although she grew up in a happy and loving family environment, almost from the start of Marya's life there was a cloud over the Sklodowskis. Bronislawa contracted tuberculosis, and never allowed herself to kiss the children for fear of infecting them. When Marya was 5 and 6 her mother had to spend long periods away from home, in Austria and then in France, convalescing in the clean air that provided the only hope of a cure for TB at the time. It would be to no avail, and her mother would die from the disease in 1878 when Marya was just 10.

In 1873, in the middle of Bronislawa's 'cure' and with the Sklodowski budget stretched to the limit, Wladislaw lost his job and was replaced by a Russian. This meant they also lost their apartment, and were forced into several short-term tenancies before settling in a house big enough for Wladislaw to take in a handful of boarders, forming a tiny private school. At about the same time he lost what remained of his own capital through an unwise investment in a scheme promoted by a brother-in-law. From now on there was no doubt that the Sklodowski children would have to find their own way in the world, with no parental help – except for receiving every encouragement to obtain a good education.

The 'school' that was home to the children in the 1870s (though they attended outside schools) was noisy and very overcrowded. The overcrowding may have been a factor in the tragedy that struck the family in 1876, when an epidemic of typhus ran through Poland. Both Zofia (known as Zosia) and little Bronislawa (Bronya) contracted the disease; Bronya recovered, but Zosia died, aged 14, on 31 January. Marya was 8 when she lost her eldest sister; a little more than two years later, she saw her mother, who died at the age of 42, buried.

The surviving Sklodowski children, clearly realizing that education was their only hope of success in life, pursued their goal in earnest. Moving on from private schools for young children to the *gymnasium* system, first Jozef, then Bronya, and then (in 1883, at the age of 15) Marya graduated at the top of their class and received a gold medal. Helena, the fourth of the surviving siblings, was an able student, but short of the standards set by the other three, and followed in the family tradition of working in education.

For a boy who graduated top of the class, even a Polish boy, there were further educational opportunities. Jozef went on to medical school, at Warsaw University, and became a doctor. But there were no university places for women in Poland under Russian rule. Girls like Bronya and Marya might dream of travelling abroad to study, to Paris, perhaps – but without money it would be no more than a dream. And the family had no money.

For some reason, though, Wladislaw allowed his youngest daughter one major indulgence before she would have to settle down to earn a living. He let her take a year off, visiting friends and relations in the country, and simply relaxing and enjoying herself. It is possible that this was just a reward for her achievements at school; there is also a suggestion that she had been ill, perhaps through overwork, or with a continuing depression following the deaths of her sister and mother. Whatever the reason, this was probably the only time in her life that Marya enjoyed complete freedom and idleness.

By the time Marya's idle year was over, her father, now in his fifties and nearing retirement, had given up taking in boarders and moved to a small apartment, though he was still teaching. Like her sisters, she tried to earn some money by private tuition, but without much success. A year later she found a post as governess with a wealthy Warsaw family, and hated every minute of it. But she kept up her academic ambitions, both through private reading and through participating in the 'Flying University', a clandestine organization which met at various sites around Warsaw to provide some sort of further education for women in her circumstances. This was in 1885; by 1889, there were more than a thousand young women regularly attending its classes.

Sometime in her 17th year, Marya came up with a plan. Both Marya and Bronya dreamed of going to Paris to study, and hoped to be able to save enough money to do so before they became too old. Bronya, two years older than Marya, had enough saved to survive on for a year – but she wanted to become a doctor, and the course lasted for five years. At the rate they were going, she would be 30, at least, before she could begin her studies.

Marya suggested that they pool their resources. Bronya could leave for Paris immediately, while Marya got another job as a governess, with a more agreeable family. She would send all the money she could spare, and Wladislaw would do what he could to help, so that Bronya could finish her course. Then, the newly qualified doctor could support Marya while she went to the Sorbonne.

The first part of the plan was for Marya to get a job as a governess. She found a position with a family in a village about a hundred kilometres north of Warsaw, paying her 500 roubles a year, plus her keep. She set out on 1 January 1886, a few weeks after her 18th birthday, to start her new life. Today that would be no distance at all, but in 1886 it involved a train journey followed by a five-hour ride in a horse-drawn cart. She was as cut off from her friends and family as if she had already moved to Paris, as Bronya, with the promised help from Marya and their father, was now able to do.

Marya made a success of her job, playing the part of governess and establishing friendly relations with the family – to such an extent that they actively supported her when she came up with a (strictly illegal) scheme to teach some of the peasant children to read and write in Polish. Her main task was to teach the younger daughter of the household, aged 10 at the time Marya joined it, for four hours a day. She also taught the older daughter, a girl her own age who had not had the benefit of a *gymnasium* education, for three hours. And then she would spend up to two hours teaching the peasant children. In her spare time (!) she read widely, and developed, for the first time, a strong interest in scientific subjects, preparing herself as best she could for the time when she could follow Bronya to Paris.

But during her time as governess, Marya also experienced a hurtful snub. The eldest son of the family was a mathematics student, a year older than Marya, at Warsaw University. During one of the vacations, the two of them fell in love and planned to marry. But his parents – her employers – absolutely refused to allow it. Marya might be good enough to educate their daughters and be treated as *almost* one of the family, but she was not good enough to marry their son. In spite of her humiliation she stayed in her post, aware of her promise to Bronya, intensifying her own private study of physics, mathematics and chemistry, but counting the days until Easter 1889 when her contract would end.

By then, Marya's financial prospects, at least, had started to improve. Early in 1888, Wladislaw had become eligible for a state pension – but the terms allowed him to teach as well, and he had obtained the post of director of a reform school at Studzienic, near Warsaw. It was an unpleasant job, which therefore carried a relatively high salary, and he was able to take over the entire financial commitment to Bronya, offering to send her 40 roubles a month. Bronya's immediate reaction was to tell him to hold back 8 roubles each month for Marya; together with Marya's own earnings, this enabled her to begin to build up the fund she would need for her own studies.

After her stint in the countryside, Marya was delighted to find a job for a year as governess with a family in Warsaw. She still seemed years away from fulfilling her dream of going to Paris, which had taken on an air of unreality in her mind. But in March 1890, Bronya, who had fallen in love with a Polish exile in Paris, a medical student now in his final year, Kazimierz Dluski (who was ten years her senior), wrote to her sister with dramatic news. The couple intended to marry as soon as he had qualified, while Bronya still had a year of her own course to complete:

> We shall stay another year in Paris, during which I shall finish my examinations . . . If you can get together a few hundred roubles this year you can come to Paris next year [she means the next academic year] and live with us, where you will find board and lodging. It is absolutely

necessary to have a few hundred roubles for your fees at the Sorbonne. The first year you will live with us. For the second and third, when we are no longer there, I swear Father will help you . . .

But Marya seems to have been so conditioned by her years of sacrifice that she could not at first accept that her dream was coming true. She wanted to stay in Warsaw to help Helena and Jozef financially; most of all, she had promised to live with her now elderly father. She had dreamed her dream for so long in isolation, that she couldn't now accept it as a reality.

The problem was overcome when Bronya and Kazimierz decided to stay on in Paris after Bronya had graduated. This allowed Marya to spend a year in Warsaw with her father, who had now properly retired. She gave private lessons, attended the Flying University during the height of its activities, and was actually able, for the first time in her life, to have access to a laboratory and carry out experiments for herself, with the help of a cousin, Jozef Boguski, who was working at the Museum of Industry and Agriculture in Warsaw. And all the while her siblings were encouraging her to take the plunge and go to Paris.

All in all, the extra year in Warsaw was undoubtedly beneficial to Marya's future, enabling her to improve her science, take stock of her life, and prepare for her greatest adventure. In November 1891, the month she turned 24, Marya at last set off for Paris, travelling in the cheapest class on the three-day journey by rail, wrapped in blankets for warmth. Symbolically, she registered at the Sorbonne as 'Marie' Sklodowska – a sign of her eagerness to be assimilated into her new environment.

After all that she had been through to achieve her dream, Marie had no intention of wasting the opportunity. Given her background and the extent to which she was self-taught, there were inevitably gaps in her knowledge. In addition, though her French was very good, what she had learned in Poland was not quite the same as the everyday French spoken by her fellow students and the professors at the Sorbonne. The solution to both problems was to immerse herself in her work, spending all her time at the Sorbonne, speaking and listening to French, studying hard, and returning to her sister and brother-in-law's apartment only for the evening meal and a few hours of sleep.

Soon she found that even this semblance of a normal life was unsuitable. The Dluski apartment was a meeting place for Poles, full of distractions from work; the young doctor was frequently called out to his patients in the middle of the night, disturbing her sleep; and when none of this was going on, Kazimierz played the piano. The apartment was also an hour's journey from the Sorbonne, wasting two hours a day of valuable working time.

Within a few months Marie had moved out to live in (literally) a garret, at the top of six flights of stairs, in the Latin Quarter. It was too hot in summer and, as Marie later recalled in her *Auto-biographical Notes*, too cold in winter. She lived on three francs a day (for *everything*, including books, rent, fuel and clothing, not just food), immersed herself in her work, and survived on tea and bread-and-butter. A boiled egg was a treat; the occasional meal with Bronya and Kazimierz may literally have saved her from starvation. There is little more to say about her student life at the Sorbonne because all she did was work, eat the minimum amount required to keep her going, and sleep the minimum amount required to stop her from collapsing in the street.

The result was spectacular. In July 1893, after two years at the Sorbonne, the foreign girl who had become seriously interested in science only while working as a governess in a Polish village, came first in the examinations for the *license es sciences* – the equivalent of a modern Master of Science degree. The success meant that, back in Warsaw for the summer, she was awarded an Alexandrovitch Scholarship, worth 600 roubles, for an outstanding Polish student wishing to work abroad. It was enough to enable her to return to Paris and take the *license es mathematiques* exam in 1894, after one more year of study; this time she came second. A few years later, when Marie carried out her first paid work, she saved 600 roubles from her fee and, to the astonishment of the administrators of the Alexandrovitch Foundation, sent it to them to repay what she had always regarded as a loan, so that they could use it to give another young student the same opportunity she had had.

Marie started that extra year in Paris intending to return to Warsaw with her qualifications at the end of it, become a teacher, and look after her father. But in the early spring of 1894 something happened that would change her life: she met Pierre Curie. She was 26; he was 34.

Pierre Curie has, down the years, received two kinds of bad press. One of these false versions of the story portrays him as a second-rate physicist who rode to glory on the apron strings of his wife. The other (a kind of backlash against the first calumny) sees him as the genius behind Marie: it gives him all the credit for their joint work, and relegates her to the role of a kind of lab assistant. Both these extremes are utter nonsense. The scientific partnership between Pierre and Marie was very much one of equals. A key factor was that their skills were complementary, so that they did not duplicate each other's work but produced a whole that, as we shall see, was genuinely greater than the sum of its parts. But it is true that Pierre was a successful scientist before he met Marie, and that the work he carried out in other areas (especially magnetism) would have ensured him a place in scientific history even if he had never investigated radioactivity. Marie, by contrast, was in a sense a one-project woman, whose place in the scientific pantheon rests entirely on her work in radioactivity. So it is worth a brief digression to set Pierre Curie in his scientific context in the mid-1890s.

Pierre was born in Paris on 15 May 1859. He was the son of a doctor, and had an elder brother, Jacques, who also became a successful scientist. Their father, Eugène, was an unusual man. He had fought on the barricades, and been wounded, during the unsuccessful revolution of 1848; and in 1871, during the unrest of the Paris Commune, he turned his apartment into an emergency hospital, treating victims of the street-fighting who were sought out and brought to him by Jacques and Pierre. Eugène's anti-establishment feelings ran strongly enough for him to refuse to send his sons to school, instead teaching them at home himself. For Pierre, in particular, this was a spectacular success, firing an early enthusiasm for science (though leaving large gaps in his classical and literary education). At 14, Pierre was provided with a tutor to give his mathematics a more solid foundation; at 16, he entered the Sorbonne;

at 18 he passed his *license es sciences* examinations and started work as an assistant in the physics department at the Sorbonne. By now, Jacques was working in a similar position in the mineralogy department at the university, and soon the brothers, who were always close friends, started to carry out research together.

Through their experimental studies of symmetry in crystals, the brothers discovered that when some crystals are squeezed they release electricity, a phenomenon now known as piezoelectricity. Pierre was 21 (Jacques was four years his senior) when they published news of their discovery, which they developed into an apparatus for measuring tiny electric currents by turning the trick around to measure the pressure produced in a crystal by the application of a small electric current. The work formed the basis of Jacques's doctoral thesis, but Pierre, as unconventional as his father, didn't bother to write up a thesis of his own.

In 1883, Jacques moved on to work at the University of Montpelier, and got married. Pierre became the head of the laboratory at the new École Municipal de Physique et Chimie Industrielles (EPCI), where he taught and (with some difficulty at first) continued his research. Jacques was always convinced that this move damaged Pierre's career in research, since he had to spend valuable time setting up the laboratory from scratch (made no easier by the fact that although the EPCI was a new institution, it existed in old buildings) and organizing the teaching. But Pierre seems to have been happy as a teacher, glad of the freedom the position gave him to work and teach in his own way, unconcerned with academic status or fame. The theoretical work on the principles of symmetry that Pierre Curie carried out in the 1880s is highly regarded, and has applications today in many fundamental areas of physics – even our modern understanding of particle physics, for example, is largely based on symmetry principles.

In the early 1890s, Pierre turned his attention to a practical study of magnetism. The work (which eventually formed the subject of his own doctoral thesis) concerned the way in which the magnetic properties of different materials depend on temperature. He found, among other things, that a dramatic change in the magnetic properties of some substances takes place at a critical temperature (different for different substances) which is still known as the Curie temperature, or Curie point. The theoretical explanation of the effects that Pierre investigated had to await the development of quantum theory, after his death; but his observations still provide the experimental basis for our understanding of magnetism. Had he not met Marie, and had he lived long enough, Pierre Curie might well have won a Nobel prize for this work.

By the time he did meet Marie, Pierre was very highly regarded in scientific circles – at least, outside France. In his own country he received little recognition, even though his work had caught the attention of luminaries such as Lord Kelvin, then the British grand old man of science, who made a point of seeking Pierre out and discussing his work when Kelvin visited Paris. That lack of recognition was in no small measure because Pierre was a self-effacing man who not only did not seek honours but actively avoided them. When the director of the EPCI suggested putting him up for an academic award, he refused to allow his name to go forward. Although he would have been ideally suited to the role of professor at the Sorbonne, he dreaded the thought of the procedure of being a candidate for such a post, in competition with others, and having to go through the formal process of soliciting support for his candidature.

It was magnetism that brought Marie and Pierre together. At the beginning of 1894, she had been commissioned by the Society for the Encouragement of National Industry to carry out a study of the magnetic properties of different kinds of steel. This was to be her first piece of research, but she had no suitable laboratory in which to carry it out. She mentioned the problem to some Polish friends, the physicist Jozef Kowalski and his wife, who were in Paris on honeymoon. Kowalski knew about Pierre Curie's work, and arranged a meeting between Marie and Pierre to see whether Pierre could provide the laboratory space that Marie needed. The pair, both dedicated scientists, hit it off immediately, and soon Pierre was sending her presents – a copy of his paper 'On symmetry in physical phenomena: Symmetry of an electric field and of a magnetic field,' inscribed 'to Mlle Sklodowska, with the respect and friendship of the author, P. Curie'. He visited her tiny room, and though he had never taken much interest in prizes and awards for himself, he eagerly looked out for her exam results, to see if she would, as he hoped, be in the top three in her year. By the time she left for Warsaw in the summer, he had asked her to marry him.

This wasn't the first proposal Marie had received. There had been at least one other suitor in her last year as a student, a Monsieur Lamotte, about whom very little is known. She had had no difficulty rejecting his offer, and had it not been for Pierre she would have had few regrets about returning to Poland. But Pierre was different, not least because he was a fellow-scientist, and she recognized the power of the argument, repeated in his frequent letters, that by leaving Paris for good she would be abandoning not just him, but a promising career in science.

In the autumn Marie returned to Paris, but she still only committed herself to just one more year there while she found a suitable problem on which to work for her Ph.D. Pierre suggested that they live together, but Marie (seemingly without taking offence) refused, while she considered her future.

He talked to her of steeling himself to apply for a professorship if a vacancy arose; he offered to give up everything and move to Warsaw with her if she would marry him; he introduced her to his parents; and (surely a gesture of love, to please her) he at last wrote up his work on magnetism as a thesis, and in the spring of 1895 became Dr Pierre Curie. One result of this was that he was made a professor at the EPCI. This was a modest promotion, but one which did not involve the agonies of competitive candidature, and it did bring in a little more money – 500 francs a month, enough, just, to get married. Marie could hold out no longer. On 26 July 1895 Marie and Pierre were married at the town hall in Sceaux, on the outskirts of Paris, where Pierre's parents lived. Marie's father and her sister Helena came from Warsaw for the ceremony, joining Bronya and Kazimierz, who were still in Paris. Marya Sklodowska was now Marie Curie, and after a honeymoon summer she would settle down to research aimed at obtaining her own Ph.D.

As a treat for themselves, with money they had been given as a wedding present, the Curies purchased a pair of the latest safety bicycles ('safety' meant that both wheels were the same size, not like a penny-farthing), with the still novel pneumatic tyres, and spent much of the summer on a cycling holiday, before settling, in late August, on a farm with relatives from both sides of the family. Cycling was to remain a passion with them, and during vacations they would head off by train for some remote part of France, unload their machines and ride where fancy took them. Pierre painstakingly learned a little Polish, and on the rare occasions they were separated he would add endearments in Marie's own language to the letters he sent her.

Back in Paris after their honeymoon summer, Marie settled down to studying for her teaching certificate (while continuing her work on magnetism in steels), giving her a profession to fall back on if required. She learned to cook, and seems to have been determined to be a good wife as well as a good scientist. Not that the science would suffer; being Marie Curie, she wanted to do both jobs to the best of her ability, even if that meant working twice as hard as anybody else. What with the new way of life, the teaching diploma, the work on steels and the fact that she became pregnant at the end of 1896, it would be late 1897 before Marie settled down to work for her doctorate.

The pregnancy was not easy, and she suffered severely with sickness and dizzy spells. At the same time Pierre's mother became ill with breast cancer. So in July Marie went off on holiday on her own, the first time the couple had been separated for two years. Pierre joined her in Brittany a month later, and they headed off on their usual cycling tour – even though Marie was eight months pregnant. The baby, Irène, was born on 12 September 1897, soon after they returned to Paris; Pierre's mother died two weeks later.

This might not seem the ideal circumstances in which to start work on a Ph.D., even today. In September 1897, though, no woman had completed a doctorate at any European university, though in Germany Elsa Neumann would soon become the first to do so.

One of the reasons why Marie, in consultation with Pierre, decided to study 'uranium rays' for her thesis was precisely because they had been neglected since Becquerel's original discovery. The director of the EPCI agreed to allow her the use of a small room (really a storage space) on the ground floor of the building. The outside wall was largely glass (single glazing, with no insulation), and the room was damp, lacked electricity and was essentially unheated. In February 1898, Marie recorded the temperature *inside* her 'laboratory' as just over 6°C. But the working space was provided free, and with Pierre in effect acting as her supervisor Marie (who had no funding for her work) was equally free to carry out her research any way she wanted, without following the guidance of a professor at the Sorbonne. So that is where she started work, just after her 30th birthday and the birth of her first child. To help with the baby, they employed a succession of young women, often Polish.

Marie's first experiments involved measuring the activity of uranium very precisely, using sensitive instruments largely developed by Pierre from his earlier work with Jacques. The radiation from uranium made air conduct electricity in its vicinity, and the strength of this effect provided a measure of what would now be called the radioactivity of the sample (this ionization of the air which allows it to conduct electricity is the principle behind the Geiger counter). She found that the activity depended only on the amount of uranium present, not what form it was in or even what compound it was in. What mattered was the actual mass, and therefore the number of atoms, of uranium present. The activity seemed to be a property specifically of uranium *atoms*, whatever environment or form they were in – a crucial insight at that time.

If uranium atoms could produce this kind of activity, could others? Surprisingly, to modern eyes, nobody had carried out a systematic investigation to search for activity in other substances. Marie set about doing this, intending to work through all known chemical substances in her methodical way. She hit the jackpot almost immediately, on 17 February 1898, when she tested a sample of pitchblende, the ore from which uranium itself was extracted. The pitchblende turned out to be *more* active than uranium itself! The general tests continued, and exactly a week later she found that thorium, an element discovered in 1828, is also more active than uranium. As it happened, unknown to the Curies the radioactivity of thorium had been discovered a few weeks earlier, by a German physicist, Gerhardt Schmidt. But the discovery of the extreme activity associated with pitchblende was new. Marie decided that there was only one explanation. Pitchblende must contain, in addition to uranium, a previously unknown but much more active element.

The discovery was so dramatic that in March 1898 Pierre Curie essentially abandoned his own research and joined forces with Marie. Their aim was to isolate this new element from pitchblende, and determine its physical and chemical properties. At about this time, Pierre (and Marie) suffered a major disappointment. A vacancy for a professorship had come up at the Sorbonne, and, as he had promised her he would, he had applied. But the post went to a younger researcher, Jean Perrin. It was some consolation that Marie's first paper on radioactivity was presented to the Académie des Sciences on 12 April. It was read by Gabriel Lippmann, Marie's teacher at the Sorbonne, because neither Marie nor Pierre were members of the Académie. It contained the evidence that radioactivity is an atomic phenomenon, and the suggestion that the activity of pitchblende 'leads us to believe that these minerals may contain a much more active element than uranium'.

Efforts to isolate the new element continued in the ill-equipped and unhealthy laboratory at the EPCI. The Curies soon found evidence for not one but two new elements, each much more active than uranium. One of these substances had similar chemical properties to bismuth, so standard techniques for separating bismuth out of pitchblende also separated and concentrated this element with the bismuth. In a similar way, the other new element was associated with barium. The Curies concentrated their initial efforts on the element that accompanied bismuth in chemical reactions, and on 18 July Henri Becquerel himself read the first joint paper by the Curies on radioactivity to the Académie.

It was in this paper that they introduced the term radio-activity (with the hyphen); and they gave the new element the name polonium 'after the name of the country of origin of one of us'. This was not just the sentimental gesture it is sometimes portrayed as, but an overt political act. After all, officially there was no such country as

Poland. By giving the new element this name, Marie risked being exiled from her homeland by the Russian authorities. (Unfortunately, polonium later turned out to be a short-lived element, produced by the radioactive decay of uranium, and losing half its activity in just 138 days, which limits its usefulness.) Also in July, the Curies began to receive recognition for their work when the Académie des Sciences awarded Marie the Gegner Prize, worth 3,800 francs, for her work on magnetism and radioactivity.

And then, as usual, the Curies went off on their summer vacation. That year there were also farewells to be said, as Bronya and Kazimierz had decided to leave Paris at last and settle in the Austrian part of Poland. Kazimierz was exiled from Russian Poland because of his anti-Russian activities as a young man, but he had never been involved in any specifically anti-Austrian political activities, so he was accepted there.

In the autumn they returned to their work, trying to separate the second radioactive element from pitchblende. They were able to concentrate it enough in a solution for its unique fingerprint of spectral lines, unlike that of any other element, to be measured, and gave it the name radium; the discovery was announced at a meeting of the Académie on 26 December. Unlike polonium, radium stays active for a relatively long time, with a half-life of 1,620 years, which makes it useful in medical and other applications.

With clear proof that the new radioactive elements existed, there were now two paths to follow, and the Curies chose one apiece. Pierre would concentrate on investigating the phenomenon of radioactivity, and trying to find its cause; Marie would continue with the chemical side of the work, trying to extract the new elements from pitchblende in large enough quantities for their distinctive chemical and physical properties to be analyzed. It was a task she was ideally suited for, being stubborn, determined, used to working for long hours under difficult conditions and, more than most people, used to the idea of waiting, if necessary, for years to achieve her dream.

It turned out that in order to extract even tiny traces of radium from pitchblende literally tonnes of raw material had to be processed in order to obtain a fraction of a gram of radium. And the

Curies had to buy the raw material with their own money. Pitchblende itself was expensive, because uranium salts were used in industry to make glazes; but the residue, after uranium had been extracted, was almost worthless and could be bought cheaply. They still had to arrange, and pay, for the material to be transported from Austria, where it was mined, to Paris.

And they – or rather Marie – still had to process it. The award of the Gegner Prize was not enough to raise her esteem sufficiently for a real laboratory to be provided, but the EPCI did have an abandoned wooden shed, with a leaky roof, that nobody else wanted. So that was where Marie beavered away for the next three years, extracting radium in tiny quantities from a mountain of pitchblende residue. The conditions of dirt, cold, damp and what can only be described as industrial pollution were so bad that they would probably not have been permitted in a factory even at the beginning of the twentieth century. In addition, the Curies were exposed to quantities of radiation that would terrify any modern scientist – by 1902, their apparatus and the laboratory were so contaminated that they would (to the Curies' delight!)

literally glow in the dark; their notebooks from this period are still regarded as too dangerously radioactive to handle for long, and are kept locked away in radiation-proof containers.

Working under these appalling conditions, and with Pierre still carrying a heavy teaching load, the story makes for a romantic tale of struggle, as enshrined in Eve Curie's biography of her mother, and which is now part of modern folk-lore. Inevitably, more recent historians and biographers, more distanced from Marie, have tended to emphasize that the Curies were not entirely ignored by the French establishment, and that after Marie's first award of the Gegner Prize (she was to receive it twice more) they were given further significant sums from one source or another: 20,000 francs in 1902, 10,000 francs in 1903, and lesser awards. But note the dates – this recognition came *after* the bulk of the back-breaking work to isolate radium. And the real turning-point in the Curies' fortunes came not through recognition in France, but through the offer of a professorship for Pierre in Geneva.

The offer came in 1900, with the promise of a fully equipped laboratory, two assistants and a post for Marie (like many people at the time, the Swiss were unable, or unwilling, to understand that Marie was the leader in the radioactivity work). It is hardly surprising that his first response was to accept. But during their summer vacation in 1900, the Curies had a change of heart and decided to stay in Paris. They had recently moved to a pleasant house in the suburbs, where Pierre's father lived with them (the rent, just over 4,000 francs a year, puts the size of the awards they received into perspective), and they decided that the upheaval of a move, as well as bringing disruption to the family, would disrupt Marie's work on isolating radium.

But some good did come out of the Swiss offer. Stung into action by the thought that they might lose the Curies altogether, the French authorities found a junior teaching post for Pierre at the Sorbonne – in addition to his existing work at the EPCI. At about the same time, in the late summer of 1900, Marie became a teacher at the École Normale Supérieure in Sèvres – a first-class teacher-training college for women. She was the first woman to lecture there. Both jobs eased the Curies' financial situation, but also increased their work-load. They worked too hard, ate too little and (though nobody realized it) were beginning to suffer from radiation poisoning. Pierre, in particular, began to have problems with what was thought to be rheumatism. But they still took their proper family holidays, including visits to Warsaw.

In March 1902, Marie completed the purification of one-tenth of a gram of radium from the tonnes of pitchblende residue she had started with. It was enough to be analyzed chemically, and to have its atomic weight determined, locating it in the periodic table of the elements. She sent the news to her father in Warsaw, who received her letter a few weeks before he died, on 14 May, at the age of 70. Over the next year, free from the labour of isolating radium, Marie at last settled down to write up her work in the form of a Ph.D. thesis; she became Dr Marie Curie in June 1903.

The next few years were the heroic time for radium, in the way that X-rays had been all the rage in the second half of the 1890s. The key to the surge of public interest was the discovery that the radiation from radium could kill cancerous cells. It was to be a long time before it was properly appreciated that it also killed healthy cells, even though Marie, Pierre and other people who worked with the purified substance had suffered frequent burns from handling it.

But 1903 would be a mixed year for the Curies. Marie, to the delight of both of them, was pregnant at the time she completed her dissertation. But in August 1903, in the fifth month of the pregnancy, she miscarried, and spent much of the rest of the year convalescing. In a letter to her brother Jozef she describes a persistent slight cough, influenza and a diagnosis of anaemia, together with a general feeling of fatigue. Pierre suffered similar symptoms, plus his 'rheumatism'. Very probably, at least some of these ailments, and perhaps the loss of the baby, were caused by radiation. In December, though, there was wonderful news: Pierre and Marie, together with Henri Becquerel, were awarded the Nobel Prize for Physics for their work on radioactivity. The value of their share of the award was 150,000 kronor (about 70,000 francs), enough to solve all their immediate financial problems (and to give generous help to friends and relations), and meant that Pierre could cut down on his teaching. But it also meant that they were now to some extent public property – in particular Marie, the first woman to win a Nobel prize. Most important of all, though, the establishment at the Sorbonne suddenly decided to create a special professorship for Pierre, without any need for him to go through the torture of competition for the post. At first, the offer made no mention of laboratory facilities, and Pierre turned it down; the omission was quickly rectified and the terms changed to provide for both a lab and a job for Marie as laboratory chief.

Alongside all this, Pierre's own research continued. He had found, for example, that radium releases an astonishing amount of heat – enough for one gram of it to heat a gram of water from freezing point to boiling point in one hour. And there seemed no end to this activity, which would go on for hour after hour after hour. This discovery, and similar observations by other scientists, threw the scientific world into confusion at the beginning of the twentieth century. It looked like something for nothing, and with no understanding of where the energy could be coming from, doubts were expressed about the law of conservation of energy, one of the most sacred cornerstones of science. The mystery would be solved only when it became clear that in radio-activity a tiny amount of matter is being converted into energy, in line with Albert Einstein's famous equation $E = mc^2$; but that equation would not be published until 1905, and not fully understood for decades.

At the beginning of 1904, though, Pierre was 44 years old, and Marie was 36. Neither of them made any major contributions to science after they had received their joint Nobel prize. This is often the case: first, very few people have it in them to do more than one exceptionally good piece of scientific work; secondly, the best original work is usually done by young people; and thirdly, the award itself almost always brings with it status and an increasing commitment to admin-istration and teaching rather than research. All three factors applied to the Curies. From now on, the development of an understanding of radio-activity, and through that an understanding of atoms and nuclei, would be in the hands of a younger generation of physicists, notably Ernest

Rutherford. And there were special reasons why the Curies made no more groundbreaking scientific discoveries.

In the spring of 1904, Marie found that she was pregnant again. After the disappointment of the previous year she took great care during this pregnancy, even giving up her teaching at Sèvres for the time being, and gave birth to another daughter, Eve, on 6 December, almost a month after her 37th birthday. For the time being family pushed science into the background, but Marie was back teaching at Sèvres in February 1905. While Marie was pregnant, Pierre was being installed at the Sorbonne and preparing his lectures for the coming year. In June 1905, all the courses safely delivered, they travelled to Stockholm for Pierre to give the long-delayed (because of illness and pregnancy) speech to the Swedish Academy of Science to mark the award of their Nobel prize, and in the summer they enjoyed a glorious holiday in Normandy, accompanied by Marie's sister Helena and Helena's 7-year-old daughter, who visited them from Poland.

By the end of 1905 the Curies were settling into a new routine, with Pierre working at the

Sorbonne, and Marie dividing her time between the children, the lab and Sèvres. The only real cloud on the horizon was Pierre's continuing fatigue, and sometimes depression. In April 1906 they took a few days off at Easter to enjoy the fine spring weather in the country with the children. It was a happy time, and their future together as a family looked bright. But on 19 April, Pierre was dead.

He died crossing a road in Paris on a rainy day, when he slipped and fell under the wheels of a heavy, horse-drawn waggon. The top of his skull was crushed by the left rear wheel of the vehicle. Marie was devastated.

But life went on. A month after Pierre's death Marie was offered the chance to succeed him, with the same duties but the lesser title of *charge de cours* (the Sorbonne still couldn't quite bring itself to make a woman a professor, but she was the first woman to teach there). She gave her first lecture on 5 November; and in the spring of 1907 moved to Sceaux, to the west of Paris, away from the house filled with reminders of Pierre. Pierre's father, Eugène, stayed with the family, and helped to provide a father-figure for the girls. But even

Eugène Curie could not live for ever, and he too died, on 25 February 1910.

Marie Curie's story might have ended soon after. For a time, she was plunged into renewed gloom. When Eugène was buried in the family tomb at Sceaux, she had insisted that the grave-diggers first remove Pierre's coffin, then return it to the grave on top of Eugène's, so that when her turn came Marie's coffin could lie directly above Pierre's. This morbid planning for her own death, and her general demeanour, seemed to her friends to indicate that she was ready, at the age of 42, to give up her grip on life. But within a few months she was restored, and became as much her old self as she ever would be again. The cure was love – what seems to have been a passionate affair with a fellow-scientist and professor at the Sorbonne, Paul Langevin, who was nearly five years younger than her, and married (albeit unhappily).

The affair, which went on for well over a year, could not be kept secret, and became a public scandal when one of the more disreputable news-papers of the day got hold of it. The story broke on 4 November 1911 (by which time Langevin had been living apart from his wife for some time), at a particularly inconvenient time since the Nobel Committee was on the brink of awarding Marie a second Nobel prize, this time in chemistry (for her work on isolating radium) and on her own. That news was released on 7 November, but passed with the minimum of comment in the French newspapers. On 23 November, another scandal sheet published extracts from letters from Marie to Langevin (they had got the letters from Langevin's wife), with an accompanying article which, among other things, denounced Langevin as a 'boor and a coward'. This led to Langevin challenging the writer to a duel, which took place on 26 November in the Bois de Vincennes. Happily for the combatants (though slightly reducing the impact of the story) both of them saw sense at the last minute, and refused to fire their pistols.

In spite of these difficulties – or perhaps, given her character, because of them – Marie made a point, this time, of attending the Nobel ceremonies in Stockholm along with the other recipients on 10 and 11 December, even though she was unwell. It has been suggested (for example, in Robert Reid's biography *Marie Curie*) that this second Nobel prize was deliberately awarded by the Nobel Committee, which had got wind of the Langevin affair, as a gesture of solidarity. This suggestion rather misses the point that the committee has never been subtle enough for that kind of gesture. If you agree with Reid that Marie did not deserve two prizes for what was in effect the same work (an argument which carries some force when you remember that Einstein only ever got one prize), it is much easier, in the light of their decisions down the years, to believe that the 1911 Committee simply made a mess of the award. And the argument that the scandal may have biased them in her favour totally ignores the fact that Svante Arrhenius, a senior member of the Swedish Academy of Sciences, had written to her before the ceremony suggesting that she might stay away from the presentation, because the Academy would have been unwilling to award her the prize had they known the full details of the affair. In her reply, Marie stressed that she saw no connection between her scientific work and her private life, and her determination to travel in spite of her illness was undoubtedly reinforced by this opposition.

That determination nearly killed her. Soon after she returned to Paris, Marie was rushed to hospital. She was eventually, some weeks later, operated on for a kidney problem, but recovery was slow and took the best part of two years, with further spells in a sanatorium – not least because she first insisted on getting back to work as soon as she felt slightly better. And in the midst of all this, the affair with Langevin was definitely over. She did little work, and travelled a lot (often under an assumed name), staying with friends. The one professional bright spot was that a Radium Institute was, at last, being built to provide a home for her work and that of her successors, in the Rue Pierre Curie. The enduring domestic bright spots were her two healthy and happy daughters.

Once again, you might think that the story of Marie Curie's life is ready for the slow fade. But once again her life was transformed, this time by war. Aged 46 when the First World War broke out, and recently recovered from a serious illness (not to mention the trauma of the Langevin affair), she nevertheless determined to find an active role to play. When she found out from Becquerel that there was a shortage of X-ray equipment and people to operate it at the hospitals near the front, she knew what she had to do. Almost single-handedly she extracted funding from charitable institutions such as the Red Cross and adapted X-ray equipment to make portable radiology units, carried in cars donated by rich women at Marie's insistence (and she could be very insistent).

Twenty such radiology cars were put into service, together with 200 fixed radiology stations. Marie travelled with one of the cars (and sometimes drove it) herself, operating the X-ray equipment at field hospitals to locate shell fragments in the bodies of wounded soldiers. According to Eve Curie's biography, the total number of men examined by the 220 X-ray stations established by Marie exceeded a million. Irène, 17 in 1914, worked with her mother's team as a radiographer during the war, and together they trained some 150 other radiographers. And at the end of the war, another of Marie's dreams was realized – Poland became an independent nation once again.

After the war, Marie was more of a figurehead than a scientist. She had her Radium Institute, but ironically the thing it really lacked was enough radium for its research and medical work. With Pierre, she had decided from the outset not to take out any patents on the process for refining radium, and not to seek commercial profit from their work, which meant that others, particularly in the United States, had reaped the commercial benefits. The situation was at least partly rectified through the efforts an American journalist, Marie Meloney (known as 'Missy'), who interviewed Marie Curie and campaigned to raise funds to purchase a gram of radium for her Institute. In return, Marie travelled to America in 1921 to tour and be put on public display, and officially take charge of the radium. She did not enjoy the experience, but it was worth it for a gram of radium.

Back home, though she had cataracts in both eyes and became almost blind, Marie continued to run the Radium Institute, where Irène Curie now worked, and where, in the early 1930s, Irène and her husband Frédéric Joliot would carry out the work that would bring them the award of a Nobel prize. But Marie also took long holidays, and was often tired.

Marie's last great project was to use her influence to get another Radium Institute, where radiation therapy would be used to treat cancer, established in Warsaw, the capital of the newly free Poland. Her great ally in this work was her sister Bronya, who handled practical matters at the Polish end; Marie's major contribution, apart from donating her name, was to tour America once again in 1929 to help the fundraising drive for a gram of radium for Warsaw. The Radium Institute of Warsaw was officially opened on 29 May 1932, in Marie's presence – on her last visit to her birthplace.

Two years later, in May 1934, she paid her last visit to the laboratory in Paris, going home early because she had a fever. No doctor knew quite what to make of her illness, and she was sent off to the fresh air of a sanatorium in the Savoy mountains, more in hope than expectation of a recovery. She died on 4 July, at the age of 66, of what is now recognized as having been leukaemia, caused by her long exposure to hard radiation. The wonder is that she lived so long.

Afterword

As we have said, Marie Curie was the right person in the right place at the right time. She was determined, hard-working, a good scientist, and helped by a first-class collaborator. Because she was a woman she encountered difficulties that she would not have encountered had she been a man. But because she was a woman, once she had overcome those difficulties and achieved what she did achieve, she became the stuff of legend. Perhaps she received even more recognition, especially posthumously, than she would have received had she been a man.

Now, more than sixty years after her death, it is easier to look back and see Marie Curie as a great woman rather than a great scientist. This is one reason why we have given so much space to the story of her early life and struggle, and relatively little to her life and work after 1906 (the fact is, she did little scientific work of any significance after 1906). We hope that the story we have told convinces you that she was a remarkable woman. But just how important was her scientific work?

You can still find Marie Curie described as 'the greatest woman scientist', but that is plain ridiculous (if forced to make odious comparisons, we would give that honour to the geneticist Barbara McClintock). The discovery of radioactivity was certainly a major turning-point in science, but that was made by Becquerel. The slightly belated discovery that uranium is not the only radioactive element was also an important step forward, but one that had already been made by Gerhardt Schmidt, before Marie's work. She was more thorough, and made the most of her opportunities, but following Schmidt's report of the activity of thorium it would surely have been no more than a matter of months before somebody carried out the kind of tests that led to the discovery of polonium and radium.

All of this work was crucial, of course, in developing an understanding of the nature of the atom and its nucleus. But that development from the discoveries made by the Curies was largely carried out by others, initially by Rutherford. There is nothing in the story of radioactivity that you could point to and say, in all honesty, 'without Marie Curie we would never have known that'. At most, she speeded up the discovery process by a year or two. If you think this is too damning a criticism, remember that it applies to most scientific developments. Charles Darwin almost lost his claim to be the father of the theory of natural selection by delaying publication for so long that he was nearly pre-empted by Alfred Russel Wallace. If we say that Marie Curie was at the top of the second division of scientists, we hope her fans will not be too offended. Her story is certainly well worth telling as a story, regardless of her importance on the scientific stage.

A brief history of science

All science is either physics or stamp collecting.

Ernest Rutherford

c. 2000 BC	First phase of construction at Stonehenge, an early observatory.
430 BC	Democritus teaches that everything is made of atoms.
c. 330 BC	Aristotle teaches that the Universe is made of concentric spheres, centred on the Earth.
300 BC	Euclid gathers together and writes down the mathematical knowledge of his time.
265 BC	Archimedes discovers his principle of buoyancy while having a bath.
c. 235 BC	Eratosthenes of Cyrene calculates the size of the Earth with commendable accuracy.

AD 79   Pliny the Elder dies while studying an eruption of Mount Vesuvius.

400   The term 'chemistry' is used for the first time, by scholars in Alexandria.

c. 1020   Alhazen, the greatest scientist of the so-called Dark Ages, explains the workings of lenses and parabolic mirrors.

1054   Chinese astronomers observe a supernova; the remnant is visible today as the Crab Nebula.

1490   Leonardo da Vinci studies the capillary action of liquids.

1543   In his book *De revolutionibus*, Nicolaus Copernicus places the Sun, not the Earth, at the centre of the Solar System. Andreas Vesalius studies human anatomy in a scientific way.

c. 1550   The reflecting telescope, and

	later the refracting telescope, pioneered by Leonard Digges.
1572	Tycho Brahe observes a supernova.
1580	Prospero Alpini realizes that plants come in two sexes.
1596	Botanical knowledge is summarized in John Gerrard's *Herbal*.
1608	Hans Lippershey's invention of a refracting telescope is the first for which there is firm evidence.
1609–19	Johannes Kepler publishes his laws of planetary motion.
1610	Galileo Galilei observes the moons of Jupiter through a telescope.
1628	William Harvey publishes his discovery of the circulation of the blood.
1643	Mercury barometer invented

by Evangelista Torricelli.

1656   Christiaan Huygens correctly identifies the rings of Saturn, and invents the pendulum clock.

1662   The law relating the pressure and volume of a gas discovered by Robert Boyle, and named after him.

1665   Robert Hooke describes living cells.

1668   A functional reflecting telescope is made by Isaac Newton, unaware of Digges's earlier work.

1673   Antony van Leeuwenhoeck reports his discoveries with the microscope to the Royal Society.

1675   Ole Roemer measures the speed of light by timing eclipses of the moons of Jupiter.

1683 Van Leeuwenhoeck observes bacteria.

1687 Publication of Newton's *Principia*, which includes his law of gravitation.

1705 Edmond Halley publishes his prediction of the return of the comet that now bears his name.

1737 Carl Linnaeus publishes his classification of plants.

1749 Georges Louis Leclerc, Comte de Buffon, defines a species in the modern sense.

1758 Halley's Comet returns, as predicted.

1760 John Michell explains earthquakes.

1772 Carl Scheele discovers oxygen; Joseph Priestley independently discovers it two years later.

1773 Pierre de Laplace begins his work on refining planetary orbits. When asked by Napoleon why there was no mention of God in his scheme, Laplace replied, 'I have no need of that hypothesis.'

1783   John Michell is the first person to suggest the existence of 'dark stars' – now known as black holes.

1789   Antoine Lavoisier publishes a table of thirty-one chemical elements.

1796   Edward Jenner carries out the first inoculation, against smallpox.

1798   Henry Cavendish determines the mass of the Earth.

1802   Thomas Young publishes his first paper on the wave theory of light.
Jean-Baptiste Lamarck invents the term 'biology'.

1803	John Dalton proposes the atomic theory of matter.
1807	Humphrey Davy discovers sodium and potassium, and goes on to find several other elements.
1811	Amedeo Avogadro proposes the law that gases contain equal numbers of molecules under the same conditions.
1816	Augustin Fresnel develops his version of the wave theory of light.
1826	First photograph from nature obtained by Nicéphore Niépce.
1828	Friedrich Wöhler synthesizes an organic compound (urea) from inorganic ingredients.
1830	Publication of the first volume of Charles Lyell's *Principles of Geology*.

1831   Michael Faraday and Joseph Henry discover electromagnetic induction. Charles Darwin sets sail on the *Beagle*.

1837   Louis Agassiz coins the term 'ice age' (*die Eiszeit*).

1842   Christian Doppler describes the effect that now bears his name.

1849   Hippolyte Fizeau measures the speed of light to within 5 per cent of the modern value.

1851   Jean Foucault uses his eponymous pendulum to demonstrate the rotation of the Earth.

1857   Publication of Darwin's *Origin of Species*. Coincidentally, Gregor Mendel begins his experiments with pea breeding.

1864   James Clerk Maxwell formulates equations describing

all electric and magnetic phenomena, and shows that light is an electromagnetic wave.

1868   Jules Janssen and Norman Lockyer identify helium from its lines in the Sun's spectrum.

1871   Dmitri Mendeleyev predicts that 'new' elements will be found to fit the gaps in his periodic table.

1887   Experiment carried out by Albert Michelson and Edward Morley finds no evidence for the existence of an 'aether'.

1895   X-rays discovered by Wilhelm Röntgen. Sigmund Freud begins to develop psychoanalysis.

1896   Antoine Becquerel discovers radioactivity.

1897   Electron identified by Joseph

Thomson.

1898 Marie and Pierre Curie discover radium.

1900 Max Planck explains how electromagnetic radiation is absorbed and emitted as quanta. Various biologists rediscover Medel's principles of genetics and heredity.

1903 First powered and controlled flight in an aircraft heavier than air, by Orville Wright.

1905 Einstein's special theory of relativity published.

1908 Hermann Minkowski shows that the special theory of relativity can be elegantly explained in geometrical terms if time is the fourth dimension.

1909 First use of the word 'gene', by Wilhelm Johannsen.

1912 Discovery of cosmic rays by

Victor Hess. Alfred Wegener proposes the idea of continental drift, which led in the 1960s to the theory of plate tectonics.

1913   Discovery of the ozone layer by Charles Fabry.

1914   Ernest Rutherford discovers the proton, a name he coins in 1919.

1915   Einstein presents his general theory of relativity to the Prussian Academy of Sciences.

1916   Karl Schwarzschild shows that the general theory of relativity predicts the existence of what are now called black holes.

1919   Arthur Eddington and others observe the bending of starlight during a total eclipse of the Sun, and so confirm the accuracy of the general theory of relativity. Rutherford splits the atom.

1923	Louis de Broglie suggests that electrons can behave as waves.
1926	Enrico Fermi and Paul Dirac discover the statistical rules which govern the behaviour of quantum particles such as electrons.
1927	Werner Heisenberg develops the uncertainty principle.
1928	Alexander Fleming discovers penicillin.
1929	Edwin Hubble discovers that the Universe is expanding.
1930s	Linus Pauling explains chemistry in terms of quantum physics.
1932	Neutron discovered by James Chadwick.
1937	Grote Reber builds the first radio telescope.
1942	First controlled nuclear reaction achieved by Enrico

Fermi and others.

1940s   George Gamow, Ralph Alpher and Robert Herman develop the Big Bang theory of the origin of the Universe.

1948   Richard Feynman extends quantum theory by developing quantum electrodynamics.

1951   Francis Crick and James Watson work out the helix structure of DNA, using X-ray results obtained by Rosalind Franklin.

1957   Fred Hoyle, together with William Fowler and Geoffrey and Margaret Burbidge, explains how elements are synthesized inside stars. The laser is devised by Gordon Gould. Launch of first artificial satellite, *Sputnik 1*.

1960   Jacques Monod and Francis Jacob identify messenger RNA.

1961   First part of the genetic code cracked by Marshall Nirenberg.

1963   Discovery of quasars by Maarten Schmidt.

1964   W.D. Hamilton explains altruism in terms of what is now called sociobiology.

1965   Arno Penzias and Robert Wilson discover the cosmic background radiation left over from the Big Bang.

1967   Discovery of the first pulsar by Jocelyn Bell.

1979   Alan Guth starts to develop the inflationary model of the very early Universe.

1988   Scientists at Caltech discover that there is nothing in the laws of physics that forbids time travel.

1995   Top quark identified.

1996   Tentative identification of evidence of primitive life in a meteorite believed to have originated on Mars.